# A Patchwork of Poetry

Paul Macklin

BookLeaf Publishing

Presentation by *BookLeaf Publishing*

Web: www.bookleafpub.com

E-mail: info@bookleafpub.com

ISBN: 9789357444279

First edition 2022

# DEDICATION

To everyone still reading.

# helpless

iridescent
dream drops –
a flooding of thoughts
puddling in my chest
fissured tears that
feel like broken fingers
raining down into the
pit of my stomach.

i can't help but feel
that everything is too hard
that everything
is a battle to be won
and a war to be lost.

# before,

before, there was a flicker of hope
a flash of the flame in my heart
the glint of the glimmer in my eyes
but age has softened my skin
stress has yellowed my teeth
and my blood has thinned my hair.

before, there was a battalion of dreams
marching on and marching on
with such fire and hubris
but the mundane is a sniper
spitting its stressed steel and
seeking its next kill –
one by one by one by one

before, it was just the same
and nothing has really changed
but like the weathering of the rock
I've lost my definition with the
winds of time coursing against
my pallid skin and dying eyes.

# confessions

i have a confession to make –

but the colour of my skin dilutes
the colour of my thoughts;
born with gold dust melanocytes
into a home where cobwebs
graced the gaps between my
parent's fingers.

There is so much to say -
but I have not
the time,
nor the humility
with which to say it.

There has been a shift -
can't you feel it?
how the words that i
spit, have suffered from
the foam of the ocean
- a saltiness rising
in the back of my throat.

i was born to become irrelevant.

strip me of my skin
let me just be me again -
a pattern of the thoughts inside
not a compartmentalisation
of the colour my skin was dyed
at a birth I didn't choose
in a land I do not love.

such a pity
that my city of cells
spills out in such a
displeasing
tone

of voice
unburdened by the past
a past that does not exist –
within my lifetime
this preconception of
my privilege
but rather a history and
heritage
coloured by
the skin I'm in.

such soft and silent
gasps for help
could carry
hot air balloons

across the horizon
until I'm left with nothing
to say
and we all
crash land
into the
sea

# true story

when i was young i bit off my tongue
just a useless lump that hung
and bled
a swinging pendulum of
my flesh
hanging by a thread
it has since been sewn back on
but my voice has not
and so my words
remain unsaid.

# nimbus

cumulus cloud winter
fogging up my head –
a forever of thought
tiptoeing around the
inevitable flotsam
spattered across
infinite sands;

how hands clamber
at each chimerical
vestibule – an hour glass
scarring as each grain
scratches impossibly
through my
thoughts.

one day
the time will come
where there will be no
time
and
no dream
left to
live

for.

and
so
my
heart
will be
found, hanged
from its arteries
a noose bound
to clouds
that wash
the feelings
away in pitter
patter stains
of rain.

# a field of flowers

Dark moon eyes
shivering shell
watching
I'm watching
I'm going to hell.

Silver-stained name,
a rapture of tooth;
a smile
a window of love.

I'll never.
No, I'll never.
Keep speaking as the heart keeps beating
and keep it coming, keep it flowing
keep those words going.

Offer a prayer
a voice, a word
of your choice.

And flowers take me
in the moonlight
by the glint of their eye
and the size of their hearts.

# an ocular flutter

This is impractical -
this cough of love
and ash-laden tongue
given only for receiving.

I follow your fingernails
as they bend in at the
keystroke.

I taste the apology
in my mouth
like some languid
creature, resting its
neck across my teeth -
a monumental guillotine
of yellowed ivory.

An ocular flutter
in pixel perfect poetry -
it is the peacock feather
to my heart.

# , and he stepped
# from below the sea.

whispering into conch shells
'here, have your ocean back'
a pinch of the skin and salt
kissing the rise of your cheeks.

I miss the days where I could
dismantle my mouth into
red ribbons and obsidian snowflakes -
nowadays a futile attempt at abstraction;
a coin for words spoiling a page;
purple waves in cautious fonts.

If one day the sun does not
rise in your world, reach up and
cut the cloth of night -
lest the curtain rise
and the blackness hover
immortal.

# ennui

That blackness, ripe
in sorry circles - tumbling
down through the inky mists
of sea water that make up my
cavernous gut.

An empty pit, an enormous void
of heart. That kick, that candle -
that swift crease of the cheeks,
it has been missing for some time now.

Raven,
why do you sit upon my shoulder,
ungainly,
feathers flayed,
idly pecking out
my eyes.

Out of sight
and out of time,
there is no excuse for my naivety.

There is no excuse at all.
I'll lick these wounds,

and mend
my wings,
and one day maybe I'll
fly again.

# gilding the throne

Every time I wander westward
I hold a gun into the air
I couldn't –

You're diving off buildings in the
hope of flight, in the hope
of something resembling life.

And when strings play
symphonies to
the sympathy of my bones -
I'm one worry too much
for the attention of the throne.

Off with his head, and
out with his heart! And
every time I travel westward
I see a new way to stop
and an old way to start.

# how to draw a heart

atomic heart, do you hear me?
river soul and bloodless scythes
darkness collapsed and moths inside
the riddle of a riddle of a love in tides of
electric.

blossom heart, can you hear me?
I'm seeking you next to me; open artery
of earthquake symmetry and I can't see
the echo of an echo of a love in tides of
electric.

Windswept monument; a pretence ego
a weathered birth and caustic nerve
withering roots within the starless sky -
can you dream me into two?

And if I set myself on fire,
just what will you do?
Watching me melt away.
I've got nothing to lose.

Yeah, watching you watching me.
No, I've got nothing to lose.

# scurrilous

Under the weight of
a thousand suns
we have contemplated
the soft verges of river banks
and the dormant things
that settle beneath them.

We are unforgiving and
tormented by these
creatures,
so soft
and subtle
that they scurry from our lives
in a whirlwind of possibility.

I am whole
when I think of you
and the colours of your skin,
the echoes of moles
surviving that sun,
hung in the sky like a
great luminous bulb swinging
from a ceiling
cracked and fragmented by time and
coated in a frost of dust.

Your heart beats and the lights
flicker, the floorboards shake
and the river continues to pump dark red
poison into my mouth.

# spilling blanks

effluvial thought -
amidst lemon sky seasons while
a gun-like tongue all
stripes and stars settle in
cannon -
one after another
after another
after another
right into your
petty little
opinions.

keep coiled, young cobra
keep reams of paper
spilling out of the press,
hot and steamy
like the soft
and shimmering surface
of a distant star.

so distant
so remote
that any bright
moment
is a landmark

unseen
but in dog-eared
postcards
with the words
"see you later"
scribbled in red
scrawl, right
across
the
back.

# untangle

I've been busy watching
how the wind bends,
loud and dangerous,
hovering above the world
like a chandelier of lies.

And as we become feverous,
as we become embroiled
in each other's kaleidoscope love,
the sky rains down in
a beautiful deceit -
a precipitation of little
white lies as soft
as a lover's kiss
against the nape,
of your neck.

# auroras

Show me your secrets
show me your true face
behind the makeup of love.

That smile so painted.
Those seaborn lips
sudden and promised,
often open, almost tasteless.

Your skyborn words were
louder in ink.

It is
in retrospect
that my night
misses your light.

Tumbling copper rust
waved ardently
in the sky and
swam through
my void.

And if I could go back
I'd still ask you to lift

the veil.

It would be my gift
were I forever
haunted by Libras.

# crave

a hammer of soul
on the window pane
because my heart is rain
my mind the trace of it
against the sun.
ineffably ardent,
inexplicably sorry,
indescribably sad.
but sadness is nothing.
nothing but the hunt
for something in
a dark place
without candles.

oh
how i craved
that rock of body
against mine
in perpetual
motion
in ardent
thrust
and
touch

oh. Oh.

perhaps i am just carried
away by the undertow
of song.
perhaps i am
illiterate for love.
but love is nothing.
nothing but the hunt.
nothing but the candle.

# dance

in another life
tonight might have
been the night.
i might have shed
my soul for
that smile.
i might have rid these
crimson sleeves
for your lunar skin.
oh my sweetest
empyrean, i love -
You.
regardless of these
artefacts, my
daydream days and
sail away love set
new horizons, my
makeshift heart
in kaleidoscope spectrum
approaches the conundrum
of your silken smile.

Dance love. Dance.
a beat belongs here
in the space between us.

# home

cupped earth in my hands
and breathed in the
recollection of petrichor.
an open door of city,
a city of open doors.
you'll find me in
the manifolds,
you'll find me in
the sea.

# hyprocisy

an acre of stars
in fist shaped thump
lingers on the intersection
of my muse. a bruise
of stellar noise in
flamboyant hiss
my volcanic heart
at the surface of my spine
holding that
knife
in place.

# islands

It has been some time
since I last allowed my
skin to meander -
awash of worry and sickness.
I fear that I have become the
very thing I feared the most
and that islands have risen
on my forearms, around which
veins must flow to forgotten
peninsulas where my heart
once thrummed.

It has been some time
since my eyelashes stroked your thighs
since my voice touched your insides.
I'm folded in dead romance,
filled with ancient song
and punch drunk from old, familiar stars.
There is no one like us in adulthood.

# slow now

a riddle;
how might we
walk the same
road, with
our backs always
facing,
yet reach the
same destination?
a little tug here
a little tug there
it seems to me
that we aren't
going anywhere.

amble along  star shine
greet my moon with your sun
i'll piss away the light you shared
flirt with the planets
in their irregular orbit.

i'm so used to disappointing you
that your scorn and tears
no longer hurt.
no. they act as an anchor
harbouring my heart

in the shallow waters of a dirty sea.
will i follow you?